DATE DUE

SO-AJM-374

Joining
Materials

Chris Oxlade

Crabtree Publishing Company

www.crabtreebooks.com

Crabtree Publishing Company

www.crabtreebooks.com

Editors: Hayley Leach, Adrianna Morganelli, Michael Hodge
Senior Design Manager: Rosamund Saunders
Designer: Ben Ruocco
Photographer: Philip Wilkins

Photo credits: Phil Degginger/Alamy p. 13; David R. Frazier Photolibrary, Inc/Alamy p. 12; Emil Pozar/Alamy p. 11; Jiri Rezac/Alamy p. 17; Jim Craigmyle/Corbis cover, p. 20; Laura Dwight/Corbis p. 25; Charles Gupton/Corbis p. 22; Saed Hindash/Corbis p. 6; Jacqui Hurst/Corbis p. 21; Andy Bullock/Getty Images p. 18; Luis Castaneda Inc/Getty Images p. 15; Phil Degginger/Getty Images p. 16; Laurence Dutton/Getty Images p. 19; Lester Lefkowitz/Getty Images p. 3, p. 9, p. 14; Davies & Starr/Getty Images p. 8; Arthur Tilley/Getty Images p. 24; Dorling Kindersley p. 7, p. 10, p. 23; Philip Wilkins pp. 26-27.

Activity & illustrations: Shakespeare Squared pp. 28-29.

Cover: A carpenter joins wood using a miter joint.

Title page: A welder joins a metal beam together.

The publishers would like to thank the models Philippa and Sophie Campbell for appearing in the photographs.

Because of the nature of the Internet, it is possible that some website addresses (URLs) included in this book may have changed, or sites may have changed or closed down since publication. While the author and publisher regret any inconvenience this may cause the readers, no responsibility for any such changes can be accepted by either the author or the publisher.

Library and Archives Canada Cataloguing in Publication

Oxlade, Chris
     Joining materials / Chris Oxlade.

(Working with materials)
Includes index.
ISBN 978-0-7787-3639-4 (bound).--ISBN 978-0-7787-3649-3 (pbk.)

     1. Materials--Juvenile literature. 2. Materials--Experiments--Juvenile
literature. 3. Joints (Engineering)--Materials--Juvenile literature.
I. Title. II. Series: Oxlade, Chris. Working with materials.

TA403.2.O94 2007   j620.1   C2007-904321-6

Library of Congress Cataloging-in-Publication Data

Oxlade, Chris.
     Joining materials / Chris Oxlade.
         p. cm. -- (Working with materials)
     Includes index.
     ISBN-13: 978-0-7787-3639-4 (rlb)
     ISBN-10: 0-7787-3639-3 (rlb)
     ISBN-13: 978-0-7787-3649-3 (pb)
     ISBN-10: 0-7787-3649-0 (pb)
     1. Materials--Juvenile literature. 2. Materials--Experiments--Juvenile
literature. 3. Joints (Engineering)--Materials--Juvenile literature. I. Title.
II. Series.

     TA403.2.O95 2008
     620.1'1--dc22   2007027420

Crabtree Publishing Company

www.crabtreebooks.com   1-800-387-7650

Published in Canada
Crabtree Publishing
616 Welland Ave.
St. Catharines, Ontario
L2M 5V6

Published in the United States
Crabtree Publishing
PMB16A
350 Fifth Ave., Suite 3308
New York, NY 10118

Published by CRABTREE PUBLISHING COMPANY
Copyright © **2008**

Published in the United Kingdom in 2006 by Wayland, an imprint of Hachette Children's Books
The right of the author to be identified as the author of this work has been asserted by him.

CONTENTS

Words in **bold** can be found in the glossary on page 30

Joining materials

Everything around you is made up of materials. Everyday materials include paper, plastic, metal, and glass. We use these materials to make objects, such as this book.

← *Gluing is just one of the ways that we join pieces of material.*

Glue, screws, nuts, bolts, nails, and zippers are all things that we use to join materials. We use them to make joints between pieces of material. The way that we make a joint depends on the materials that we want to join.

↑ *This person is joining two pieces of wood with a screw.*

7

Nuts, bolts, and screws

Two pieces of material, such as wood and metal, can be joined with nuts, bolts, and screws. The bolt is put through a hole in a material, and the nut is put on the end of the bolt. Then the nut is turned. This pulls the two pieces of material tightly together.

↓ *There is a long groove around the outside of the bolt and another on the inside of the nut. The two grooves fit into each other.*

↑ *This worker is using giant nuts and bolts to hold the metal frame of a building together.*

A screw has a sharp, pointed end and a groove around the outside. When a screw is turned, the groove cuts into the material. This makes the screw dig into the material.

Sticking together

Objects such as plastic toys can be joined with glue. First, the glue is spread on the surfaces of both pieces of material. Then the pieces are pressed together firmly. When the glue dries, the pieces are stuck together.

← *Wallpaper paste is made by mixing powder with water. It glues wallpaper firmly to a wall.*

← Special glue for plastic is needed to join the parts of a plastic-model kit.

It's a fact!

Some glues come from plants and animals. For example, a glue called gum is made from the sticky liquid from gum trees.

The glue that we use for a job depends on the materials that we want to join, and on how strongly we want to join them together. For example, we can use **waterproof** glue for some jobs, such as gluing shower tiles to the wall.

Super-strong glues

Sometimes we need to glue materials together very strongly. To do this we can use super-strong glues. Some super-strong glues come in two parts. The parts must be mixed together to make the glue turn hard.

↓ *This worker is gluing down floorboards in a new house. He is using special wood glue.*

↑ *Plywood is made by joining thin sheets of wood with strong glue. It is used for making floors and walls.*

Strong glues are used to make materials called **laminates**. A laminate is made by gluing sheets of material together. Cardboard and **plywood** are laminate materials.

It's a fact!

Aircraft wings are made by gluing materials such as metal and plastic together. This makes the wings light and strong.

13

Welding metal

Welding is a way of joining together two pieces of metal. The joint is called a "weld". Both pieces of material are heated until they melt. More **molten** metal is added to the joint so that it flows into the gap and cools. This leaves a strong joint.

← This shipyard welder is joining metal. A big spark made by electricity melts the metal.

↑ *This robot is welding the metal parts of a car together.*

Many industries use welding to make objects from pieces of metal. Objects from giant cruise ships to mountain bikes are welded together. Metal beams in buildings and bridges are often welded together, too.

It's a fact!

Some plastics can be welded. For example, the edges of plastic shopping bags are welded together.

15

Soldering metal

Soldering is another way of joining pieces of metal together. A special material called "solder" is heated up until it melts. It flows between the pieces of metal. It quickly cools and joins the metals together.

← *A tool called a* **soldering iron** *is used to heat the metals.*

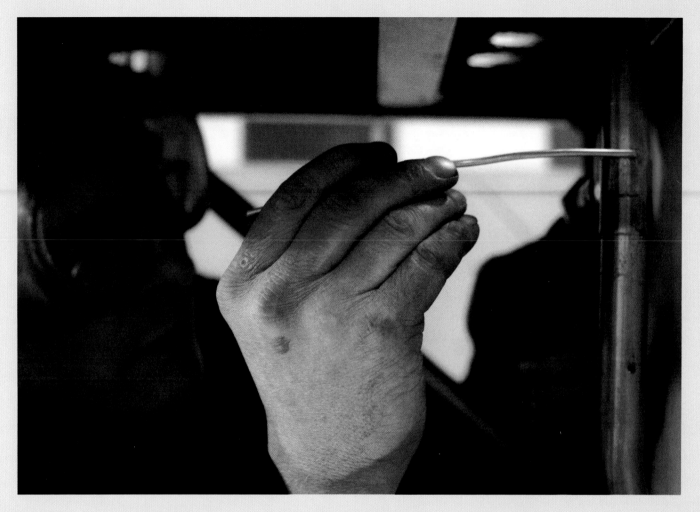

↑ *This plumber is heating the ends of a pipe with a hot flame, ready to add solder to the joint.*

Solder is used to join wires and other parts together. The solder also allows electricity to flow between the parts. Plumbers join metal water pipes with solder. The solder makes a waterproof joint.

It's a fact!

The solder used in electronics contains the metals tin and lead. This makes it melt easily.

Joining wood

We make all sorts of things from wood, including toys, ornaments, tables, chairs, cupboards, and some houses. We join pieces of wood together with nails, screws, nuts, bolts, and glue.

← *A nail is a long, thin piece of metal with a sharpened end. It grips the wood when it is hammered in.*

18

↑ *Some furniture comes with the screws, nuts, and bolts needed to put the parts together.*

The method that we use to join pieces of wood often depends on how neat the joint must look. Nails are used for fences and sheds. Glue and screws are used for good-quality furniture, because they give a neat finish.

19

Wood joints

Carpenters are craftspeople who work with wood. Carpenters normally use special joints between pieces of wood. They cut away wood on each piece so that the pieces lock together. This makes a strong, neat joint.

← This carpenter is making a drawer. The joint that he is using is called a "dovetail joint".

↑ *This picture frame has a joint at each corner.*
The joint used is called a "miter joint".

Some wood joints slot together. The end of one piece of wood slots tightly into a hole in the other piece of wood. This makes a strong joint.

It's a fact!

Hundreds of years ago, carpenters built huge ships from wood using joints like miter and dovetail joints.

21

Joining soft materials

Some materials, such as fabrics and paper, are soft and flexible. We use glue, metal staples, and thread to join soft materials together. We also use adhesive tape. Tape is made up of a plastic strip with a layer of glue on one side.

← *This girl is using adhesive tape to join pieces of wrapping paper together.*

↑ *Thread is used to stitch two pieces of fabric together.*

We join pieces of fabric together with thread. The thread passes backward and forward through the layers of fabric. This makes a line of stitches.

It's a fact!

Stitching can make a very strong joint. Safety **harnesses** and **parachutes** are held together by strong stitching.

Temporary joints

We often need to join two pieces of material for a short time so that we can take them apart again. This is called a **temporary** joint. For example, sticky note pads are designed to stick to a desk and then be peeled off again.

↓ *The glue on an adhesive bandage makes a temporary joint. The bandage can be pulled off again.*

↑ *These paddles are covered with tiny hooks. They make a temporary joint with the furry ball.*

Many clothes have temporary joints. The joints allow you to put clothes on and take them off easily. For example, a coat has a zipper down the front that joins the two sides together. Buttons can also be used to join fabrics temporarily.

See for yourself!

Flour-and-water glue

Make your own glue using everyday materials.

What you need		
plain flour	spoon	salt
water	bowl	sieve
cup	airtight container	

① Pour about 1/4 cup (60 mL) of plain flour into a bowl.

② Fill the cup with water. Slowly add the water to the flour. Keep mixing so that there are no lumps. Sieve the glue if there are some lumps.

②

③ Add a few pinches of salt to the glue. This will stop mold from growing in it. You have made flour-and-water glue.

④ You can make the glue thicker by boiling it in a pan for a few minutes. Ask an adult to do this for you. Let the glue cool before you touch it.

③

⑤ Store the glue in an **airtight** container. You can use the glue to stick paper together.

Papier-mâché head

Use your flour-and-water glue to join newspaper to a balloon.

What you need

newspaper
flour-and-water glue or
  wallpaper paste

large paintbrush
balloon

① Tear plenty of strips of paper about 1 inch (3 cm) wide.

② Blow up a balloon and tie its neck.

③ Brush glue onto both sides of a strip of paper and stick it onto the balloon.

④ Add more strips until the balloon is covered with paper strips.

⑤ Let the paper dry.

⑥ Repeat this process two more times.

⑦ Prick the balloon to burst it.
The material that you have made is called "papier-mâché". It is like a laminate material, built up of layers of paper and glue. The papier-mâché head is now ready to decorate.

27

Picture this!

Create your own picture frame

See how glue joins materials together when you turn a CD jewel case into your own picture frame!

What you need
empty CD jewel case
pencil
construction paper
photograph
scissors
craft supplies/household items
glue

1. Open the CD case and remove the front jacket, or the paper that appears inside the cover. Pop out the round tray where the CD used to sit. Then remove the back jacket.

2. Center the front jacket on your photograph. Using a pencil, trace around the jacket to make sure that your photograph is the right size for the CD case. Then cut along the pencil lines.

3. If your photograph is too small, cut a piece of construction paper the size of the front jacket. Glue your photo to the construction paper.

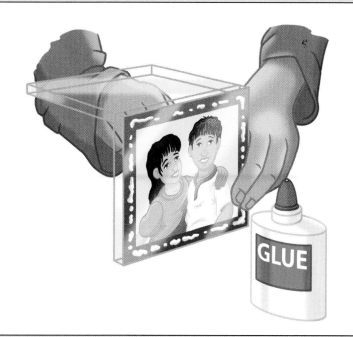

4. Turn the CD case so that the hinge is on top. Then, glue the front of your photograph to the inside of the front plastic panel. Use a thin bead of glue.

5. Use glue to join craft supplies or household items to the edge of the frame. Let the glue dry for an hour. Then open the CD case so it stands on its own, with the hinge on top.

What you will see:
Even though you can no longer see the glue, it is an important part of your picture frame! It holds the photograph to the construction paper, the construction paper to the plastic CD case, and the craft supplies to the CD case.

Glossary

airtight Stops air from getting in or out

harness A set of straps that fits around a person's body and is used to attach the person to a rope

laminate A material made by gluing thin sheets of material together

molten Heated up until melted

parachute A large piece of fabric that lets objects or people fall slowly to the ground

plywood A material made by gluing thin sheets of wood on top of each other

soldering iron A tool used to heat up solder to make joint

temporary When something is designed not to last forever

velcro A tiny hook that catches on a tiny loop to hold material together

waterproof Does not let water get through

Further information

BOOKS

How We Use: Metals/Paper/Rubber/Wood
by Chris Oxlade, Raintree (2005)

A Material World: It's Glass/It's Metal/It's Plastic/It's Wood
by Kay Davies and Wendy Oldfield, Wayland (2006)

Investigating Science: How do we use materials?
by Jacqui Bailey, Franklin Watts (2005)

WEBSITES

doityourself.com/wood/h2woodjoints.htm
Pictures of all the different ways of joining wood

www.diydata.com/materials/nails/nails.php
Which nails are used for different jobs

PLACES TO VISIT

American Museum of Science and Energy, Tennessee
www.amse.org

The Children's Museum of Science and Technology, New York
www.cmost.com

The Discovery Center for Science and Technology, California
www.discoverycntr.org

Index

All of the numbers in **bold** refer to photographs.

Printed in the USA